IMPROVING
WITH
AGE

The Best is Yet to Come

PEGGY ANDERSON

Glendale Heights, IL 60139

Compiled by Peggy Anderson

Cover Design by Design Dynamics

Published by Great Quotations, Inc.

Library of Congress Catalog Card Number : 98-075786

ISBN: 1-56245-366-1

Printed in Hong Kong

Dedicated to those who believe

that it's not a matter of counting

the years – but making the

years count.

Youth is a gift of nature, but age is a work of art.

Judy Barry

*Age is a
matter of mind; if
you don't mind, it
doesn't matter.*

The aging process
is alot like grapes,
some turn to vinegar
but the best turn
to wine.

*Wrinkles are only
the bypaths
of many smiles.*

The longer we live
the more we learn it
is not who has the
most - it is who
makes the most of
what he has.

Smart enough to know better, old enough not to care.

*Old enough to
know my limit,
young enough to
exceed it.*

You have to climb
the mountain
to appreciate the
beauty of the view.

Age stiffens the
joints
but softens the
heart.

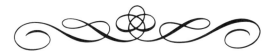

Only when your heart is covered with the snows of pessimism and ice of cynicism do you grow old.

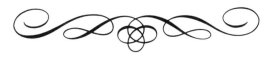

The tomorrow I worried about is better than the yesterday.

In spite of the
cost of living, it's
still popular.

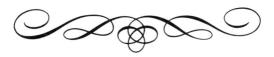

*Peace is when
time doesn't matter
as it passes by.*

Maria Schell

We grow old as
soon as we cease
to love and trust.

Madame de Choiseul

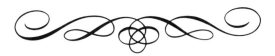

I'm old enough to know the rules and smart enough to break them.

Young at heart,
slightly older in
other places.

*As we grow
older and wiser,
we talk less
and say more.*

Growing older
we learn miracles
are great,
but they are so
darn unpredictable.

So long as the heart
receives messages of
beauty, hope, cheer,
and courage you
will be young.

*We do not
stop playing because
we are old; we grow
old because we stop
playing.*

You are young at any age if you are planning for tomorrow.

Lulline T. Hodges

Anyone who keeps the ability to see beauty never grows old.

Franz Kafka

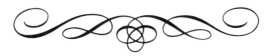

It's up to us
whether age brings
wisdom or age
comes alone.

*A man is
not old until
regrets take the
place of dreams.*

Betty Spillner

*Growing gracefully
slower of step
is only walking
nearer to God.*

Growing old wisely means making more opportunities than we find.

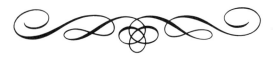

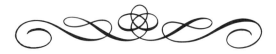

If I'd known I was going to live so long, I'd have taken better care of myself.

*Growing older
means realizing
that our life is
what our thoughts
make of it.*

*Years wrinkle
the skin, but to
give up enthusiasm
wrinkles the soul.*

Accept the changes age brings and stay alive inside.

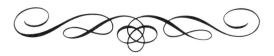

As we age we should lead our life so we wouldn't be ashamed to sell the family parrot to the town gossip.

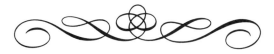

No one grows old
by merely living a
number of years.
People grow old
only by deserting
their ideas.

*Youth is the time
for the adventure
of the body, but age
triumphs of the mind.*

Logan Pearsall Smith

In this life the old believe everything, the middle-aged suspect everything, and the young know everything.

Grandchildren
are God's gift for
growing older.

Don't laugh at old age - some folks never make it.

*A man is
not old as long
as he is seeking
something.*

Jean Rostand

Age...
Is a matter of
feeling, not
of years.

George William Curtis

The tide of life
is sometimes very
rough, but each storm
ridden through makes
us a better captain of
our souls.

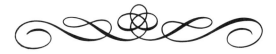

As we grow older,
we learn that the
wisest man is usually
he who
thinks himself the
least so.

Regardless of their age, most folks are not as old as they hope to be.

*Reaching my age
isn't bad at all,
especially when
you consider the
alternative.*

At my age
I don't have
to act responsible.

The secret. . .

*Find an age
and stick to it.*

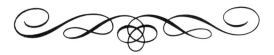

*Snow on the
roof doesn't mean
there's no fire in the
furnace.*

I'm in the prime of my life - it just takes a little longer to get primed.

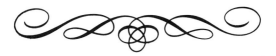

To be fifty years young is sometimes more cheerful and hopeful than to be twenty years old.

At 20 years of age
the will reigns;
at 30 the wit, and
40 the judgement.

Benjamin Franklin

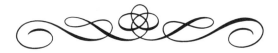

*You are
as young as your
self-confidence,
as old as
your despair.*

*Youth is the time
of getting,
middle age of
improving, and old
age of spending.*

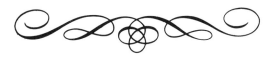

Gray hair
is the silver dust
of the stars.

Let me grow lovely, growing old—
So many fine things do;
Laces and ivory, and gold,
And silks need not be new;
And there is healing in old trees,
Old streets a glamour hold;
Why may not I, as well as these,
Grow lovely, growing old?

Karle Wilson Baker

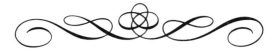

Years teach us that knowledge becomes wisdom only after it has been put to practical use.

Hardening of the heart ages people more quickly than hardening of the arteries.

Some hearts, like evening primroses, open more beautifully in the shadows of life.

Sarah Wells

We live in deeds,
not years, in thoughts,
not breaths, in feelings,
not in figures on
the dial.

G. Baily

The older we get, the more we realize - after all is said and done, more is said than done.

*A*ge does not depend
upon years, but upon
temperament and health.
Some men are born old,
and some never grow so.

Tryon Edwards

People who have the most birthdays live the longest.

*As we age
we learn riches
are mental, not
material.*

Age is like
love.
It cannot be
hidden.

*Age is the best
possible
fire extinguisher
for
flaming youth.*

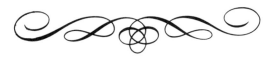

*Youth
is wasted on
the young.*

Aging...
When the onset
of wrinkles is
balanced by the
gift of wisdom.

*As we age
we realize that
we get treated in life
the way we have
trained others to
treat us.*

*As we grow older
we are alot like
plants — some of
us go to seed
while others bloom
profusely.*

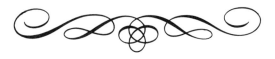

Measure your life
by the joys that it brings,
not by the years.
Measure it by the smiles
and the songs,
not by the tears.

Virginia Moody

If wrinkles must be
written upon our brows,
let them not be written
upon the heart. The spirit
should never grow old.

James A. Garfield

We neither get
better or worse as
we get older, but
more like ourselves.

Sr. Robert Anthony

Life is a gift,
to live is an
opportunity, to give
is an obligation,
and to grow old
is a privilege.

Candy Hughes

29
and holding

30
and better
than ever

40
and fabulous

50
and fantastic

60
and sensational

70

and celebrating

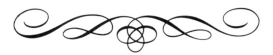

Other Titles by Great Quotations, Inc.

Hard Covers

Ancient Echoes
Behold the Golfer
Commanders in Chief
The Essence of Music
First Ladies
Good Lies for Ladies
Great Quotes From Great Teachers
Great Women
I Thought of You Today
Journey to Success
Just Between Friends
Lasting Impressions
My Husband My Love
Never Ever Give Up
The Passion of Chocolate
Peace Be With You
The Perfect Brew
The Power of Inspiration
Sharing the Season
Teddy Bears
There's No Place Like Home

Paperbacks

301 Ways to Stay Young
ABC's of Parenting
Angel-grams
African American Wisdom
Astrology for Cats
Astrology for Dogs
The Be-Attitudes
Birthday Astrologer
Can We Talk
Chocoholic Reasonettes
Cornerstones of Success
Daddy & Me
Erasing My Sanity
Graduation is Just the Beginning
Grandma I Love You
Happiness is Found Along the Way
Hooked on Golf
Ignorance is Bliss
In Celebration of Women
Inspirations
Interior Design for Idiots

Great Quotations, Inc.
1967 Quincy Court
Glendale Heights,IL 60139 USA
Phone: 630-582-2800   Fax: 630-582-2813
http://www.greatquotations.com

Other Titles by Great Quotations, Inc.

Paperbacks

I'm Not Over the Hill
Life's Lessons
Looking for Mr. Right
Midwest Wisdom
Mommy & Me
Mother, I Love You
The Mother Load
Motivating Quotes
Mrs.Murphy's Laws
Mrs. Webster's Dictionary
Only A Sister
The Other Species
Parenting 101
Pink Power
Romantic Rhapsody
The Secret Langauge of Men
The Secret Langauge of Women
The Secrets in Your Name
A Servant's Heart
Social Disgraces
Stress or Sanity
A Teacher is Better Than
Teenage of Insanity
Touch of Friendship
Wedding Wonders
Words From the Coach

Perpetual Calendars

365 Reasons to Eat Chocolate
Always Remember Who Loves You
Best Friends
Coffee Breaks
The Dog Ate My Car Keys
Extraordinary Women
Foundations of Leadership
Generations
The Heart That Loves
The Honey Jar
I Think My Teacher Sleeps at School
I'm a Little Stressed
Keys to Success
Kid Stuff
Never Never Give Up
Older Than Dirt
Secrets of a Successful Mom
Shopoholic
Sweet Dreams
Teacher Zone
Tee Times
A Touch of Kindness
Apple a Day
Golf Forever
Quotes From Great Women
Teacher Are First Class